PHYSICAL SCIENCE IN DEPTH

# HEATING AND COOLING

**Carol Ballard**

**Heinemann**
LIBRARY

www.heinemann.co.uk/library
Visit our website to find out more information about Heinemann Library books.

To order:
 Phone 44 (0) 1865 888066
 Send a fax to 44 (0) 1865 314091
Visit the Heinemann bookshop at www.heinemann.co.uk/library to browse
our catalogue and order online.

Produced for Heinemann by
White-Thomson Publishing Ltd.,
Bridgewater Business Centre,
210 High Street, Lewes,
East Sussex BN7 2NH

First published in Great Britain by
Heinemann Library, Halley Court, Jordan Hill,
Oxford OX2 8EJ, part of Harcourt Education.
Heinemann is a registered trademark of
Harcourt Education Ltd.

© 2008 Harcourt Education Ltd.
The moral right of the proprietor has
been asserted.

Editorial: Sarah Shannon, Harriet Milles and
  Harriet Brown
Design: Richard Parker and Flick, Book Design
  and Graphics
Illustrations: Ian Thompson
Picture Research: Amy Sparks
Production: Duncan Gilbert

Originated by Modern Age Repro
Printed and bound in China by South China
  Printing Company Ltd.

ISBN: 978 0 431 08106 9
12 11 10 09 08
10 9 8 7 6 5 4 3 2 1

**British Library Cataloguing in Publication Data**
Ballard, Carol
Heating and Cooling. – (Physical science in depth)
536
A full catalogue record for this book is available
from the British Library.

**Acknowledgements**
The publishers would like to thank the following for
permission to reproduce photographs:
Alamy **pp. 18** (The Print Collector), **20** (David R.
Frazier Photolibrary, Inc.), **27** (Imagebroker), **57**
(VIEW Pictures Ltd); Corbis **pp. 7** (Sergio
Pitamitz/zefa), **25** (Visuals Unlimited), **31** (Visuals
Unlimited), **42** (Comstock), **53** (Michael & Patricia
Fogden); Istockphoto **title page** (Koch Valérie), **9bl**
(Claylib), **9br** (Victor Kapas), **9tr** (Svetlana Larina),
**11**, **16** (EuToch), **17** (Oleg Prikhodko), **23** (Alysta),
**26** (Karen Harrison), **34** (Angelhell), **36** (Jason
Stitt), **38** (John Pitcher), **39** (Mary Schowe), **41**,
**48** (Jaap Hart), **52** (Nico Smit), **54** (Karina
Tischlinger), **59** (Richard Schmidt-Zuper); NASA **p.
47**; NASA Marshall Space Flight Center (NASA-
MSFC) **p. 35**; Science Photo Library **pp. 30** (Gusto
Images), **37**, **51** (Tony McConnell).

Cover photograph of lava flowing from a volcano
reproduced with permission of Science Photo
Library (Tony Craddock).

Every effort has been made to contact copyright
holders of any material reproduced in this book.
Any omissions will be rectified in subsequent
printings if notice is given to the publishers.

# Contents

Words printed in the text in bold, **like this**, are explained in the glossary.

# What is temperature?

Heating and cooling are everyday occurrences – we get hot if we exercise in the sunshine, and cold if we go out in the snow. But have you ever wondered exactly what happens to materials when they are heated and cooled, and why they behave as they do? In order to understand these things, you need to know what **heat** is, and how heat and **temperature** are different.

## WHAT IS HEAT?

Heat is a form of **energy**. Another name for heat is "**thermal energy**". Heat is measured in units called **joules**: 4.18 joules of energy are needed to raise the temperature of 1 gram of water by 1 **degree Celsius**. For larger amounts of heat energy, we measure in units called kilojoules. One kilojoule equals 1,000 joules.

## MOVING HEAT

Heat energy does not simply stay in one place. It moves from a warm place or object to a colder place or object, until they are both equally hot or cold. You can show this by putting an ice cube into a cup of hot water – the heat energy in the water will flow into the ice. The water will lose heat energy and get colder, and the ice cube will gain heat energy and get warmer. Eventually, there will be no difference between them.

## TEMPERATURE

Temperature is a measure of how hot or cold something is, and is usually measured in degrees Celsius (°C) or degrees Fahrenheit (°F). However, temperature alone is not a measure of how much heat energy a substance contains. For example, although water boiling in a kettle at 100°C (212°F) has a much higher temperature than a warm bath at 35°C (95°F), it has less heat energy.

This is because the bath contains a lot more water than the kettle. If the kettle contains 500 millilitres of water, which is heated from 15°C to 100°C, it would have 500 x 85 x 4.18 = 178 kilojoules. But if the bath contains 150 litres of water, heated from 15°C to 35°C, it would have 150,000 x 20 x 4.18 = 12,540 kilojoules!

## SCIENCE PIONEERS  James Joule: Heat energy

English physicist James Joule (1818–89) carried out important research in the study of heat. The unit used to measure energy, the joule, is named after him. He set up an experiment, as shown in the diagram below, that proved for the very first time that heat was a form of energy.
1. Weights are suspended on strings. They have **potential energy**.
2. As the weights fall, their potential energy changes to **kinetic energy**.
3. The falling weights turn the central rotor, spinning the paddles, which stir the water.
4. The temperature of the water increases. The potential energy of the suspended weights has changed into heat energy – proving they are both different forms of the same thing.

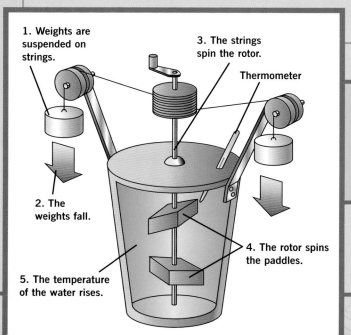

1. Weights are suspended on strings.

3. The strings spin the rotor.

Thermometer

2. The weights fall.

4. The rotor spins the paddles.

5. The temperature of the water rises.

Here you can see the apparatus Joule used for one of his famous heat experiments. The handle is turned to bring the weights to the top of the apparatus before the experiment is carried out.

# WHY MEASURE TEMPERATURE?

Knowing how hot or cold something is can be extremely useful, and can help to keep us safe. For example, a temperature gauge measures the temperature of a car engine, and warns the driver if the engine is becoming too hot. Temperature sensors in many modern cars also monitor the outside temperature, alerting the driver when it nears freezing so that they are aware there might be icy patches.

Temperature is also useful in other situations:
1. Cooks must heat the oven to the correct temperature for baking a cake.
2. Gardeners try to keep plants at the optimal growing temperature, often avoiding frosts.
3. Knowing the temperature outside helps us to dress appropriately.
4. A raised body temperature can indicate illness.

# RELATIVE TEMPERATURES

If we measure one thing against another, we are relating them – we say we are measuring one relative to the other. For example, is a sheep a big animal or a small animal? Relative to a mouse, a sheep is big, but relative to an elephant, it is small. These are relative measures.

In the same way, you can measure the temperature of one thing relative to the temperature of another. A chocolate bar might seem warm relative to an ice cream, but cold relative to a mug of cocoa!

## Did you know...?

The lowest temperature ever recorded on Earth was at Vostock Station, Antarctica, in July 1983, when the temperature dropped to –89.2°C (–128.6°F). The highest temperature ever recorded in the shade on Earth was in the Sahara Desert, Libya, in September 1922, when it rose to 58°C (136.4°F).

# YOUR BODY AND TEMPERATURE

In your skin and deep inside your body are sense organs that collect information about the temperature in the world around you and – most importantly – inside you. This information is passed to the brain via nerves, and the brain then makes you aware of how hot or cold things are. Skin can detect a temperature difference of as little as 0.5°C (0.9°F), but it cannot measure the exact temperature.

## KEY EXPERIMENT  Detecting temperature

You can investigate skin as a heat sensor by carrying out this experiment. You need a bowl of hot water (be careful – not too hot!), a bowl of cold water, and a bowl of warm water. Put one hand in the hot water and the other in the cold water. Leave them there for about one minute. Now, put both hands together into the warm water. You should find that the warm water feels hot to the hand that has been in cold water. However, the warm water feels cold to the hand that has been in the hot water. This confusion arises because the brain can only measure the temperature of one thing relative to another.

The Sahara Desert in Africa is one of the hottest places on Earth. It is so dry and hot that very little can survive here.

# THERMOMETERS

Simply comparing the temperatures of two objects does not give an accurate indication of the temperature of either of them. To obtain accurate measurements, we use instruments called **thermometers**. Thermometers all have one thing in common – they change in some way as the temperature rises and falls.

# WHY DO WE NEED DIFFERENT THERMOMETERS?

Thermometers are designed for specific uses. For example, an oven thermometer needs to be able to withstand high temperatures, and need only be accurate to within 5–10°C (9–18°F). This would be useless for monitoring the temperature of a fridge, where the temperature is much lower, and fluctuations may be by less than 1°C (1.8°F). Similarly, strong, weatherproof thermometers used for measuring soil temperature would not be ideal for measuring body temperature. There are therefore many different types of thermometer.

# LIQUID THERMOMETERS

A **liquid** thermometer consists of a tube with a scale marked along its length. Liquid inside the tube rises and falls as the temperature changes. The temperature is shown by the level of the liquid on the scale.

## SCIENCE PIONEERS  Gabriel Fahrenheit: Thermometers

Although earlier scientists had tried to make a liquid thermometer, none had been accurate or reliable. The first successful liquid thermometer was invented by German physicist Gabriel Daniel Fahrenheit (1686–1736) using mercury as the liquid in the thermometer tube. His scale measured temperatures in degrees Fahrenheit (°F) (see page 10). The Fahrenheit scale is still used in many places today.

# DIGITAL THERMOMETERS

Digital thermometers, such as those you put on your forehead to measure your body temperature, use liquid crystals. Each different number on the thermometer has a slightly different set of crystals behind it. Each set of crystals **reflects** light at a specific temperature and the number in front of them shows. As the temperature changes, different sets of crystals reflect light and different numbers show up.

# POP-UP THERMOMETERS

When cooking meat, some people use a pop-up thermometer to indicate that it is cooked. This is a tube with a spring and stick inside. The spring is held in place by a piece of metal that is **solid** at room temperature. The metal **melts** at exactly the correct temperature of perfectly cooked meat. When this happens the spring is released. The stick pops up to indicate that the meat is cooked.

These are just some of the thermometers that can be used to measure temperature.

# TEMPERATURE SCALES

Units such as millimetres and metres (or inches and feet) are used to measure length, and units such as grams and kilograms (or ounces and pounds) are used to measure **mass**.

To measure temperature, we need appropriate units of measurement. Several different sets of units, based on different scales of measurement, have been suggested by different scientists.

# FAHRENHEIT SCALE

In 1714, Gabriel Daniel Fahrenheit proposed a scale that measured temperature in units called degrees Fahrenheit (°F). It started at zero, which was the lowest temperature Gabriel could produce in his laboratory when freezing water with salt. On his scale, pure water froze at 32°F.

# CELSIUS SCALE

The Celsius scale was proposed in 1742 by the Swedish scientist, Anders Celsius (1701–44). On Celsius's original scale, water froze at 100°C and boiled at 0°C. It was reversed in 1743 by a French scientist, Jean-Pierre Cristin (1683–1755). The scale, which is used worldwide today, states that water **freezes** at 0°C and boils at 100°C.

## Did you know...?

Until 1948, the Celsius scale was known as the Centigrade scale, and its units were degrees Centigrade. This was because 1 degree on this scale is 100th of the difference between the temperatures at which water freezes and boils. "Cent" means "100", as in the words "century" (100 years) and "centipede" (100 legs). However, in 1948, it was decided internationally that the name should be changed from Centigrade to Celsius, in recognition of Anders Celsius's important work.

# KELVIN SCALE

On this scale, proposed by Lord Kelvin (1824–1907) in 1848, temperature is measured in degrees Kelvin (K). A temperature change of 1K is the same as a temperature change of 1°C (1.8°F). The difference between the scales is the starting point. The starting point on the Kelvin scale is 0K. This is called **absolute zero** and is equivalent to –273°C (–459.4°F). On this scale, water freezes at 273K and boils at 373K.

## SCIENCE PIONEERS  Lord Kelvin: Absolute zero

Lord Kelvin, whose name was actually William Thomson, was an important 19th-century Scottish physicist. He was sure that the lowest temperature possible would be reached when every **particle** in a material was motionless. He called this temperature "absolute zero" and used it as the starting point for his temperature scale.

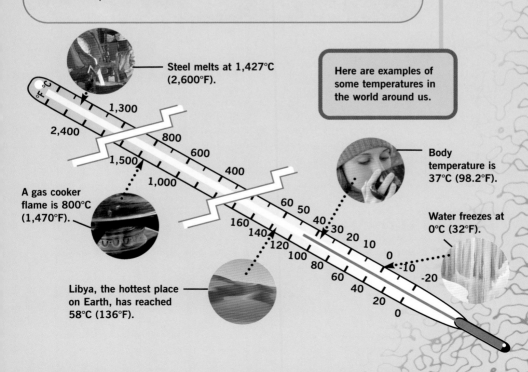

Steel melts at 1,427°C (2,600°F).

Here are examples of some temperatures in the world around us.

A gas cooker flame is 800°C (1,470°F).

Body temperature is 37°C (98.2°F).

Water freezes at 0°C (32°F).

Libya, the hottest place on Earth, has reached 58°C (136°F).

# Bigger and smaller

Solids, liquids, and **gases** all behave differently. We use a model to help us explain these differences. In our model, everything is made of billions of incredibly tiny particles that we cannot see. The particles are arranged in different ways in solids, liquids, and gases. Another name for particles is **molecules**. Each molecule is made up from even tinier pieces called **atoms**.

## SOLIDS

In solids, the particles are held together in regular patterns by attractive forces between the particles. The particles have only enough energy to **vibrate** gently in fixed positions. This arrangement means that solids cannot be squashed into a smaller space, their shape cannot be changed easily, and they cannot flow.

## LIQUIDS

The particles in liquids have more energy than the particles in solids. They can overcome the attractive forces and move around. This arrangement means that liquids – like solids – cannot be squashed into a smaller space. However, their shapes can be changed easily, and they can flow.

### Did you know...?

Each atom is made from even tinier pieces called **neutrons**, **protons**, and **electrons**. Amazingly, there are even smaller pieces, too, with strange names such as hadrons, quarks, leptons, and bosons!

# GASES

The particles in gases have even more energy than the particles in liquids. They can move around freely in all directions. This arrangement means that gases can be squashed into a smaller space. They can change shape easily, and they can flow.

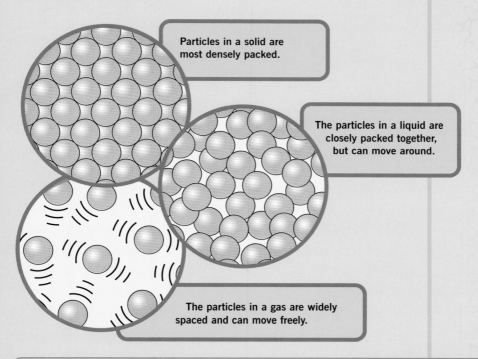

Particles in a solid are most densely packed.

The particles in a liquid are closely packed together, but can move around.

The particles in a gas are widely spaced and can move freely.

## SCIENCE PIONEERS  James Clerk Maxwell: Particles

James Clerk Maxwell (1831–79) was a Scottish mathematical physicist. He provided the foundations for many areas of modern physics. In 1860, he proposed a theory stating that temperature and heat involved the movement of particles. He worked out a formula that enabled him to calculate the fraction of gas particles that would be moving at a specific speed at a given temperature. This work became known as the "Kinetic Theory of Gases". In the same year, a German scientist, Ludwig Edward Boltzmann (1844–1906), independently came to the same conclusion, and together their work is known as the Maxwell-Boltzmann equation.

# HEATING SOLIDS

In a cold solid, each particle has only a small amount of energy, and vibrates weakly. As the solid is warmed, the particles gain heat energy and vibrate more strongly. Although the size of each particle does not change, the stronger vibrations mean that each particle needs a little more space around it. As the solid is heated, it takes up more space than when it was cold. The whole solid **expands**. The number of particles is still exactly the same, though. Therefore, the **density** of the solid (which is a measure of how tightly packed the particles are) decreases.

# COOLING DOWN

When a solid cools down, heat energy is lost. Each particle has less energy, and so vibrates less strongly. The particles need less space, and the solid gets smaller. The solid **contracts**. The density of the solid increases.

# DIFFERENT SOLIDS

Some solids expand more on heating, and contract less on cooling, than others. The table below shows by how much some common materials expand on heating.

| Material | Increase in length when 1 metre of material is heated by 1°C (in millionths of a metre) |
|----------|-----------------------------------------------------------------------------------------|
| Brass | 19 |
| Copper | 17 |
| Iron | 12 |
| Steel | 11 |
| Concrete | 11 |

# THERMOSTATS

The fact that different metals expand by different amounts can be very useful. For instance, it can help to make **thermostats**. Thermostats are used to control appliances, such as heaters, in response to the temperature around them.

Many thermostats consist of strips of two different metals joined together lengthways. These are called **bimetal strips**. The metals used are often brass and invar or copper and iron. When the strip is connected in an electric circuit, it allows the **current** to flow, and the appliance is switched on.

If the temperature rises, the metal strip heats up. Because the metals expand by different amounts, one piece of metal becomes longer than the other, and the strip bends. This moves one end of the strip out of the circuit. The current cannot flow, and the appliance is switched off.

As the temperature drops, the reverse happens. The metals contract, the strip straightens and completes the circuit, switching the appliance back on again.

A bimetal strip can be used to turn this heater on and off. One side of the strip expands more than the other when heated, breaks the electrical circuit, and turns the heater off.

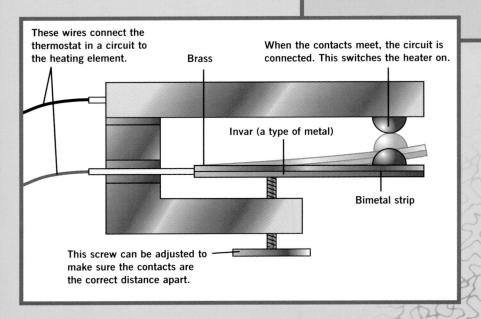

These wires connect the thermostat in a circuit to the heating element.

Brass

When the contacts meet, the circuit is connected. This switches the heater on.

Invar (a type of metal)

Bimetal strip

This screw can be adjusted to make sure the contacts are the correct distance apart.

# HEATING AND COOLING LIQUIDS

Just as heating increases the energy of particles in a solid, so heating increases the energy of particles in a liquid. Similarly, when the liquid is cooled, its particles lose heat energy.

# EXPANDING AND CONTRACTING

As a liquid is heated and its particles gain heat energy, they vibrate more strongly, and move around more freely. To do this, they need more space, and so the liquid expands. The number of particles is still the same, though, so the density of the liquid decreases. As the liquid cools, its particles lose heat energy. They vibrate less strongly, and move around less, so they do not need as much space. The liquid contracts and its density increases.

Liquids expand much more on heating, and contract much more on cooling, than solids. This is because the particles in a liquid have more energy than particles in a solid. Therefore, the increase in space needed by a liquid as it gets hot is many, many times the increase needed by a solid.

# HOW DO LIQUID THERMOMETERS WORK?

The expansion and contraction of a liquid as it is heated and cooled is the key to the way a liquid thermometer is used to measure temperatures. A liquid thermometer consists of a glass rod with a narrow channel running up its centre. At the bottom is a reservoir, called a bulb. The bulb contains a liquid. The liquid is usually a colourless alcohol called **ethanol**, with a coloured dye added so that it can be seen. A vertical scale is marked up the length of the rod.

You can clearly see the liquid in the bulb of this thermometer.

If the bulb of the thermometer is put in a hot place, the liquid inside is heated. It expands and, because there is no space left in the bulb, flows up the narrow channel at the centre of the rod. The liquid will always expand by the same amount for the same increase in temperature, and so will reach the same height in the channel. The temperature can be read from the scale on the side of the rod at the point the liquid reached. If the bulb of the thermometer is put into a cold place, the opposite happens. The liquid inside cools and contracts, flowing back down the channel.

The red liquid is hot and the blue liquid is cold. This can be seen from the two thermometers. The height of the liquid inside the thermometer in the red liquid indicates a much higher temperature than the thermometer in the blue liquid.

## KEY EXPERIMENTS  Expansion and contraction

You can use a liquid thermometer to see how quickly a liquid can expand and contract. Put the bulb of a thermometer into a bowl of hot (not boiling) water. Watch carefully and use a stopwatch to time how long it takes to stop rising. Then, put the bulb of the thermometer into cold water and time how long it takes for the liquid to fall to its original level.

# HEATING AND COOLING GASES

When gases are heated or cooled, they gain or lose heat energy in the same way as solids and liquids do. When heated, their particles gain heat energy, and when cooled, their particles lose heat energy.

# EXPANDING GASES

As a gas is heated, its particles gain heat energy, and so they vibrate more strongly, and move around more quickly. This means that they hit the sides of a container harder and more often, and so the **pressure** inside the container increases. If the gas is not in a confined space the pressure will not change, but the gas will expand.

# CONTRACTING GASES

As a gas cools, the particles lose heat energy, vibrate less strongly, and move around more slowly. They hit the sides of the container more gently and less often, and so the pressure inside the container decreases. If the gas is not in a confined space the pressure will not alter, but the gas will contract.

## SCIENCE PIONEERS  Boyle and Charles

The way in which the pressure, **volume**, and temperature of a gas are linked was worked out by two scientists, Robert Boyle (1627–91, see left) in Ireland, and Jacques Charles (1746–1823) in France. Their work and their names are remembered today in the equations known as Boyle's Law and Charles' Law.

## KEY EXPERIMENT  Expansion of air

Air is a mixture of gases. If air is heated, every gas particle in the mixture will gain heat energy, and the air will expand. When air is cooled, it will contract. This can be shown using a balloon, a bottle, a bowl of hot water, and a bowl of cold water.

Fit the open end of the balloon over the neck of the bottle. The air inside the bottle will be at room temperature, and will just fill its space. The balloon will droop down. Hold the bottle upright in the hot water. The balloon will slowly fill with air and stand up. This is because heat energy from the hot water is transferred through the bottle to the air inside. The air expands and begins to fill the space inside the balloon. The balloon stretches to provide extra space.

Next, hold the bottle upright in the cold water. The balloon will deflate. No air escapes, but instead it contracts as it loses heat energy to the cold water.

Hot water

Cold water

Warm air takes up more space (above right) than cool air (below right).

# USING EXPANSION AND CONTRACTION

We can make use of the fact that materials expand and contract as the temperature rises and falls. For example, some thermostats and liquid thermometers use this principle. However, in other situations it can be a nuisance. For example, it must be taken into account when planning buildings and other structures. Engineers need to make sure that one part of the structure does not expand and contract more than another.

## CASE STUDY  Building bridges

Bridges provide a means for people and vehicles to cross from one side of a gap to the other. The material that they are made from will expand and contract as the temperature rises and falls. If a continuous solid construction is used, the expansion and contraction would cause **buckling** and **distortion** of the bridge. The longer the bridge, the more buckling would occur. To prevent this happening, bridges are built in sections, with gaps called expansion joints between them. This allows the materials to expand and contract without causing any damage.

Expansion joint

Expansion joints, such as this one on the Golden Gate Bridge in California, USA, allow the materials to expand and contract without damaging the overall structure.

# AUTOMATIC VENTS

The temperature inside greenhouses needs to be kept within narrow limits. Automatic systems open and close windows or **vents** as the temperature rises and falls. This uses the fact that materials expand and contract in response to temperature changes.

1. When the temperature rises, the compressed liquid or gas expands.
2. This pushes the piston along its tube.
3. The piston is attached to an expandable bracket. The piston pushes the expandable bracket, which opens the vent.
4. When the temperature falls, the compressed liquid or gas contracts.
5. The piston moves back to its starting position.
6. The piston pulls on the expandable bracket, which closes the vent.

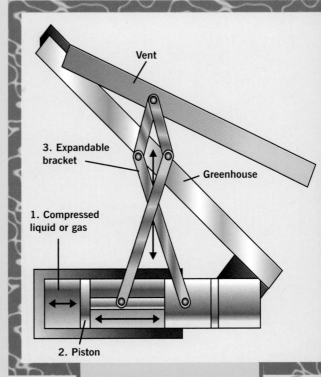

Expansion and contraction of the gas or liquid in this automatic vent system opens and shuts the greenhouse vent in response to temperature changes.

# FLASHING LIGHTS

Some flashing lights use the expansion and contraction of bimetal strips, similar to those used in thermostats. A heating coil is wound around a bimetal strip. Wires connect the heating coil to a bulb and a battery in a circuit. When the bimetal strip is cold, it connects the circuit, and the bulb and heating coil are switched on. As the coil heats the bimetal strip, it bends and disconnects the circuit. The bulb and heating coil are switched off. When the strip cools, it connects the circuit again, and so on. All that we see is the bulb flashing on and off automatically.

# Changes of state

Everything around us is a solid, a liquid, or a gas. These are called the "states of matter". When a substance is defined as a solid, a liquid, or a gas, this is the state that it is in at room temperature and under normal pressure conditions. Materials can change from one state to another if the temperature changes. For example, if solid ice is warmed, it changes state into liquid water. Changes of state can also occur if the pressure changes.

In every change of state, the only thing about the particles that changes is the amount of energy they have, which in turn affects the attractive forces between the particles. In every other respect, the particles are exactly the same as they were before the change of state.

## SOLID TO LIQUID

A material changes its state in response to a temperature change. If a solid is heated, its particles gain energy and move more. If the temperature keeps rising, the particles gain enough energy to lose their regular arrangement. The particles are able to move around and the solid has become a liquid. Changing from solid to liquid is called melting, or liquefying. This happens when a bar of hard chocolate warms and becomes runny.

## Did you know...?

Most materials contract when they freeze. Water does the opposite, though. It is the only liquid that expands when it freezes. The molecules in liquid water are held closer together than in solid ice. In ice, the molecules arrange themselves in a large, repeating pattern. The pattern results in spaces forming between the water molecules, which makes the water expand as it freezes.

## LIQUID TO GAS

If the heating continues, the particles gain even more energy. If the temperature rises enough, the particles are able to move around freely, and break loose from all of the attractive forces between them. They fill the space they occupy – the liquid has become a gas. The process of changing from a liquid to a gas is called **evaporation**. This happens when, for example, a kettle of liquid water is heated and the water turns into steam.

## REVERSING THE CHANGES

The opposite changes of state happen if a substance is cooled. As a gas is cooled, its particles lose energy and move less. Some attractive forces form between them and hold them loosely together – the gas becomes a liquid. The process of changing from a gas to a liquid is called **condensation**. This happens when, for example, steam from a hot bath hits a cold window and makes it wet and misty.

If the cooling continues, the particles lose even more energy. They move and vibrate less and less. More attractive forces form between them and eventually hold them in place in their regular arrangement as a solid. The process of changing from a liquid to a solid is called freezing, or solidifying. This happens when, for example, liquid water is put into a freezer to make ice cubes.

When water freezes it turns to solid ice. Sometimes, only a small amount of ice forms, for example on top of puddles, but huge ice formations can also occur such as the one shown in this photograph.

# THE WATER CYCLE

The processes of evaporation, condensation, freezing, and melting happen naturally all the time in the world around us. The never-ending sequence is called the water cycle:

①  Heat energy from the Sun makes the water in oceans and lakes **evaporate** (change from liquid water into water vapour).

②  The water vapour rises into the air. As it rises it cools. Eventually, it **condenses** into tiny droplets of liquid water. Millions of these droplets group together and form clouds.

③ If clouds cool, the droplets join together. Eventually they are so large that they fall to the ground. In warm weather, they fall as liquid rain. In very cold weather, the droplets freeze and fall as snowflakes or hailstones. Rain, snow, and hail falling from clouds is called **precipitation**.

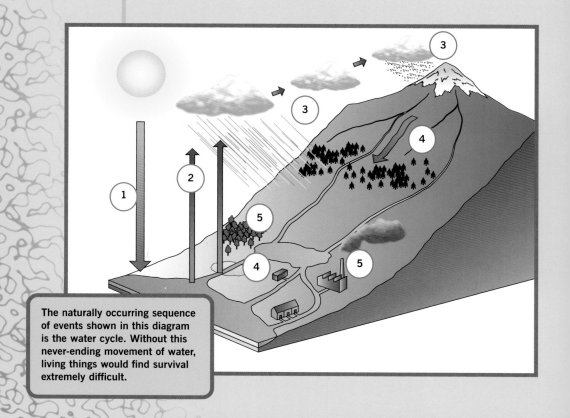

The naturally occurring sequence of events shown in this diagram is the water cycle. Without this never-ending movement of water, living things would find survival extremely difficult.

④ Some of the water that falls runs over the surface of the ground, and some soaks into the ground. Eventually, it all runs into streams and rivers, and then into the oceans, and continues the cycle.

⑤ Humans, plants, and animals use water, but it is still part of the water cycle. When humans and animals breathe out, their breath contains water vapour, which mixes with the air. Water evaporates into the air when humans and animals sweat. Waste water from homes, factories, and other buildings is cleaned and returned to the cycle. Plants take water from the ground via their roots, but any surplus returns to the air from the leaves in a process called **transpiration**.

## Did you know...?

A water crystal has a flat, regular, six-sided structure. These join together to form a snowflake. Although they can be arranged in millions of ways, every snowflake also has a six-sided structure.

Although no two snowflakes are identical, every one has a regular six-sided structure like this one.

# IMPORTANT TEMPERATURES

Changes of state happen at particular temperatures. The temperature at which a solid melts, and becomes a liquid, is known as the **melting point**. It is also called the **freezing point** because it is the temperature at which the liquid freezes and becomes a solid.

The temperature at which a liquid evaporates and becomes a gas is called the **boiling point**. Although this is also the temperature at which the gas condenses into a liquid, it is rarely called the condensation point. The melting point and boiling points are different for different substances.

# MELTING AND BOILING POINTS

If you know the melting and boiling point of a substance, you can work out whether it will be a solid, a liquid, or a gas at room temperature. If room temperature is 25°C (77°F), then any substance with a melting and boiling point higher than 25°C (77°F) will be a solid at room temperature. If the melting point is below 25°C (77°F), but the boiling point is above 25°C (77°F), the substance will be a liquid at room temperature. If both melting and boiling point are below 25°C (77°F), the substance will be a gas at room temperature.

**At the very high temperatures in this furnace, the metal changes state from a solid into a liquid. It can then be poured into moulds.**

# EFFECTS OF PRESSURE

Under normal conditions, air pushes down on everything with a force called **atmospheric pressure**. The pressure at sea level is one atmosphere, and everything else is measured from that standard point. This is the pressure at which the melting point and boiling point of a substance are measured. Changing the pressure changes the melting point and boiling point of a substance.

Above sea level, the atmospheric pressure decreases. This means that particles can escape more easily into the air and so the boiling point of a liquid is lower. For example, at the peak of Mount Everest, the highest point on Earth, the pressure is about one third of that at sea level – and water boils at just 71°C (160°F).

# MIXTURES

Mixing one substance with another will affect the melting point and the boiling point. For example, adding salt to water raises the boiling point of the water and lowers the melting point. This can be useful – food cooks more quickly in salted water because it boils at a higher temperature than pure water. Spreading salt on the ground in winter can help to prevent ice forming.

A mixture of salt and water has a lower freezing point than water alone. This is why we spread salt on roads in icy conditions.

These changes can also be useful in assessing the purity of a substance. For example, pure silver has a melting point of 1,234°C (2,253°F). If the melting point of a sample of silver is different from this, it is likely that the silver contains some impurities.

# TEMPERATURE GRAPHS

The temperature of a substance can be measured as it is heated, and as it changes state from solid to liquid, and liquid to gas. The measurements can be plotted, and a line graph drawn to give a visual image of the results.

# WHICH AXIS?

The two **variables** that need to be plotted are time and temperature. It is usual to plot the variable controlled by the scientist, called the "controlled variable", on the horizontal (x) axis. In this case, the scientist controls the time intervals at which the temperature is measured, and so time is plotted along the horizontal axis. The variable that is being measured, in this case the temperature, is plotted on the vertical (y) axis.

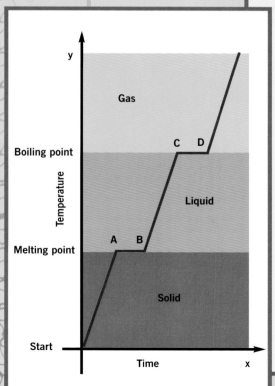

### Heating a substance

When heating a substance, a graph displaying temperature against time can be plotted. It usually looks like the graph shown here (left).

Start to A: The substance is below its melting point and is solid. The temperature rises as the substance is heated.

At A: The melting point is reached. The substance will start to melt.

A to B: The substance is melting. The temperature does not change during the melting process.

At B: Melting is complete. The substance is a liquid. The temperature starts to rise again.

B to C: The substance is above its melting point, but below its boiling point, so is a liquid. The temperature rises as the substance is heated.

At C: The boiling point is reached. The substance begins to evaporate into a gas.

C to D: The substance is evaporating. The temperature does not change during the process of evaporation.

At D: Evaporation is complete. The substance is a gas. The temperature starts to rise again.

## Cooling a substance

Particular graphic patterns are also obtained when substances are cooled.

Start to W: The substance is above its boiling point and is a gas. The temperature falls as the substance is cooled.

At W: The boiling point is reached. The substance starts to condense into a liquid.

W to X: The substance is condensing. The temperature does not change during the process of condensation.

At X: Condensation is complete. The substance is a liquid. The temperature starts to fall again.

X to Y: The substance is above its melting point, but below its boiling point, so is a liquid. The temperature falls as the substance is cooled.

At Y: The freezing point is reached. The substance begins to freeze into a solid.

Y to Z: The substance is freezing. The temperature does not change during the process of freezing.

At Z: Freezing is complete. The substance is a solid. The temperature starts to fall again.

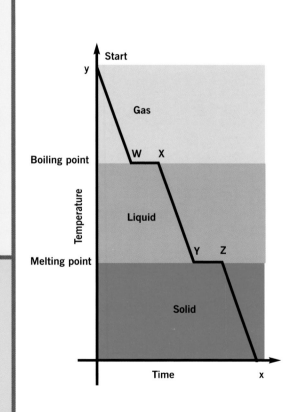

# UNUSUAL SUBSTANCES

Although most substances change state from solid to liquid, and liquid to gas, when they are heated, and change in the opposite sequence when cooled, not all do. Some substances act in a different way.

# CARBON DIOXIDE

At normal temperatures and pressures, carbon dioxide is a colourless, odourless gas. When it is cooled, it changes state – but to a solid. It does not pass through a liquid state. This change from a gas straight to a solid is called **deposition**. Confusingly, it is sometimes also called condensation, which is the term usually given to the change from gas to liquid.

If solid carbon dioxide is heated, it changes straight to the gas state, again missing out the liquid state. This change from a solid straight to a gas is called **sublimation**.

Solid carbon dioxide is commonly known as dry ice. If a block of dry ice is left at room temperature, the process of sublimation can be seen as wisps of white vapour escaping into the air around it. This misty effect can be used to create a spooky atmosphere on theatre stages.

Carbon dioxide can exist as a liquid but only at high pressures. It is usually stored as a liquid in cylinders at very high pressures.

These chunks of solid carbon dioxide are too cold to touch, so the handler is wearing protective gloves.

# HELIUM

Helium is a colourless, odourless gas. It has a lower boiling point than any other element – less than –268°C (–450°F)! At normal pressures, it cannot freeze at all, even at absolute zero.

# MERCURY

Mercury is the only common metal that is liquid at room temperature. It has a melting point of –39°C (–38°F) and a boiling point of 357°C (675°F). Mercury is the colour of silver, but unlike silver it is runny. Its chemical symbol is Hg, from the Latin word *hydrargyrum*, which means "liquid silver".

Mercury is a liquid at room temperature, forming tiny droplets such as these. If they touch, they join together to form larger droplets.

## Did you know...?

Mercury was used in early thermometers. Like any liquid, it expands or contracts as the temperature changes. Mercury was also used in barometers, to measure the atmospheric pressure. In a mercury barometer, the atmospheric pressure forces mercury from a reservoir into a narrow tube. The greater the pressure, the lower the level of the mercury. The pressure can be read from a scale on the side of the tube. As mercury is a toxic material, its use in thermometers and barometers is now uncommon.

# DEPOSITION OF WATER

Although water usually changes state from solid to liquid to gas, and vice versa, under certain conditions, it can change straight from a gas to a solid. This happens when frost forms in cold weather. Water vapour in the warm air changes straight into solid water crystals when it hits a cold surface.

# Conduction

**Conduction** is the process by which heat energy travels through solids. Heat energy passes through some solids more quickly than through others. For example, heat energy travels rapidly through metals, but more slowly through wood.

If one end of a piece of solid material is heated, heat energy passes into it. As this happens, the particles in the heated end of the solid vibrate more quickly and strongly. Because the particles are packed tightly together, they bump into neighbouring particles and the extra movements are passed on. These neighbouring particles then begin to vibrate more quickly and vigorously and in turn they bump into the particles close to them. In this way, heat energy is transferred along the length of the solid. As this happens, the solid becomes warmer throughout.

## KEY EXPERIMENT Investigating conduction

This experiment shows how quickly heat can travel through different materials by conduction. Put a small piece of butter on the end of similar objects made of different materials, such as spoons made from wood, metal, and plastic. Stand the objects in a bowl of hot water with the buttery end upwards. The heat energy from the hot water will travel through each material. When the material is hot, the butter will melt. The material through which the heat travels most quickly will be the one on which the butter melts first.

# METALS AND CONDUCTION

Metals are particularly good at conducting heat energy. This is because, in addition to their closely packed atoms, they contain free electrons. Usually, electrons are held tightly to an atom, but in metals some electrons are free to move around inside the metal.

When the metal is heated, the free electrons gain heat energy and move more quickly and vigorously. They carry the extra energy through the metal with them, passing it on when they collide with other free electrons. Heat energy moves more quickly through free electrons than through the fixed atoms. This means that heat can travel more quickly through metals than it can through materials that have no free electrons.

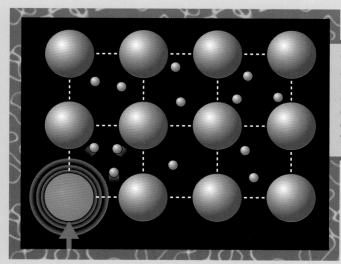

The atom at the bottom left corner of this metal is heated. The free electrons (smaller circles in this diagram) will pass the heat energy rapidly throughout the rest of the object.

## Did you know...?

The word "conduction" comes from the Latin word *conducere*. This word is made up from two Latin words, *con*, which means "together" and *ducere*, which means "to lead". It can help make sense of what is going on in conduction if you think about the particles working together to move heat energy.

# CONDUCTORS AND INSULATORS

Materials that allow heat energy to travel through them quickly and easily are good **thermal conductors**. Materials that do not allow heat energy to travel through them quickly and easily are **thermal insulators**. A good **conductor** is a poor **insulator**, and vice versa.

# MATERIALS AS CONDUCTORS

Good thermal conductors are materials in which the particles are closely packed. Heat energy is transferred quickly and efficiently from particle to particle. Materials in which particles are more spaced out are poor conductors. Liquids are poor conductors because their particles are only loosely held together. Gases, with particles free to move around randomly, are very poor conductors.

It is important to distinguish between thermal and electrical conductors. Materials that are good thermal conductors are not necessarily good electrical conductors, and vice versa. For example, diamond and graphite are both forms of carbon, but they have very different properties. This is because, although they are made from identical particles, they are arranged in different ways. Diamond is a good thermal conductor, but it cannot conduct electricity. Graphite can conduct electricity, but it is a poor thermal conductor.

Diamonds are the hardest substance on Earth. Diamonds conduct heat well, but not electricity.

## Did you know...?

Double glazing is made from two pieces of glass with air trapped in the space between them. Because air is a thermal insulator, it helps to prevent heat escaping through the glass from a warm building to the cold outside.

# MATERIALS AS INSULATORS

Insulators are the opposite of conductors. Gases are good insulators. Liquids and most solids are not as good insulators. Metals are extremely poor insulators. Some solids have spaces within their structures that trap tiny amounts of air. Air is a gas, and therefore a good insulator, so the air pockets make the solid a better insulator than it would otherwise be. Expanded polystyrene, the material used to make some disposable drinking cups, contains air bubbles and is a good insulator.

# TOUCH TEST

Feeling a material can provide a clue as to whether it is a good thermal conductor. Human body temperature is higher than room temperature. A good conductor, such as metal, will feel cold at room temperature. This is because, although it is at room temperature, it is conducting heat away from your body. A good insulator, such as wood, will not feel cold at room temperature. This is because it is not conducting heat away from your body. Both the metal and the wood are actually at exactly the same temperature. They just feel different because of the difference in the amount of heat they conduct from your body.

In the foreground, you can see the side of a spacecraft covered in black tiles. The tiles insulate it against high temperatures. They are made from silica. They disperse heat quickly and keep the inside cool. The curve of Earth can be seen in the background.

## USING CONDUCTION

Conduction allows heat energy to pass through solid materials. This can be useful in some cooking methods. It can also be a nuisance, for example, when heat is lost through a glass window. Knowing about thermal conductors and insulators can be important when choosing materials for different functions.

## COOKING BY HEAT CONDUCTION

If food is put in a pan over a direct source of heat, such as an electric ring, heat energy moves by conduction through the material the pan is made from, and into the food. For this to happen, the pan must be made of a good thermal conductor. This is why most pans are made of metal.

**Wrapping cold hands around a mug of hot liquid can soon warm them up. Heat energy moves by conduction from the hot drink, through the mug, and into your hands.**

## OTHER USES OF CONDUCTION

Conductors are good at transferring heat from one place to another. They can be used to transfer heat to something that needs to be heated, or away from something that needs to be cooled. Thermal conductors are also used in these everyday activities.

• Ironing clothes – Heat moves from the iron and into the clothes. The base of the iron must be made from a good conductor.

• Cooling computers – A computer generates heat when it is on. It could be damaged by high temperatures, so excess heat is removed by a device called a **heat sink**. This is made from a thermal conductor that conducts heat away from the **microprocessor**. The heat sink has fins that increase its surface area. This allows heat to be conducted into the air quickly and efficiently.

• Heating radiators – In many central heating systems, pipes carry hot water from a hot water tank around a house to radiators. The radiators are made from a good thermal conductor. The heat is readily conducted into the air, warming the room.

## USING INSULATION

In many everyday situations, insulators are used to prevent heat conduction. These insulators include:

• Oven gloves – The thick filling is a good insulator. It prevents heat from travelling from a hot dish into a cook's hands.

• Table mats – These are made from an insulator, such as cork or wood. They prevent heat from hot dishes travelling into the table and damaging it.

Taken using a very high-powered microscope, this picture shows fibres of a filling for a sleeping bag. The spaces inside each fibre are filled with air, which increases their thermal insulation properties.

• Cavity wall insulation – Many house walls are made from an inner and outer layer of brick with a cavity between them. Filling this cavity with an insulating foam can help to reduce heat loss through the wall.

# CONDUCTION IN THE NATURAL WORLD

The temperature of the world in which we live changes. Animals and plants need to be able to tolerate a range of temperatures. Some have developed sophisticated ways of overcoming this problem using conduction and insulation.

## BODY INSULATION

Air trapped between a bird's feathers acts as a thermal insulator. When the weather is particularly cold, birds fluff up their feathers to increase the amount of air that is trapped, and so increase their insulation. The fur of many animals also traps air in a similar way. Many, such as cats and horses, grow extra fur and hair as winter approaches, in preparation for the extra insulation needed in colder weather. This is lost in the spring, when they moult, so they do not overheat in the warmer summer months. Polar bears have to survive the icy climate of the Arctic. Their fur is made of hollow tubes that trap extra air inside.

These polar bears need very efficient insulation to allow them to survive the cold Arctic temperatures.

## Did you know...?

Snow is actually a good insulator as it traps air within it. This is why people caught in blizzards dig snow holes. They survive in "caves" dug deep into the snow, because the snow all around them provides insulation and keeps them warm.

Fat is another good insulator, and many animals that live in cold seas, such as seals and walruses, have a layer of fat called blubber. This helps to keep their body heat in when the external temperature is low. Humans do not have efficient insulating mechanisms so we need to wear clothes to keep us warm.

# KEEPING EGGS WARM

Birds lay eggs in which chicks develop until they are ready to hatch. Between the laying and hatching, the eggs must be kept warm or the chicks inside will die. Birds solve this problem by sitting on the eggs. Heat from the parent's body passes through the eggshell by conduction, and warms the developing chick and the fluids that surround it inside the egg. This keeps the egg at an ideal, constant temperature.

Insulation is provided by the nest below the eggs and by the parent bird above them. This keeps the eggs at just the right temperature for the chicks inside to develop and eventually hatch.

## CASE STUDY  Crocodile eggs

Crocodiles dig holes in the ground to make nests in which to lay their eggs. The female lays up to 50 eggs in the nest, carefully arranging them in layers with sand between each layer. She then fills the hole with sand. Sand is a good conductor. Heat energy from the Sun travels through the sand by conduction and keeps the eggs warm until the baby crocodiles are ready to hatch. If the nest gets too hot, the female crocodile splashes water on it, or drags grasses over it. Scientists have discovered that the temperature of the nest affects the sex of the babies. There are more males hatched from cool nests than from warm nests.

# Convection

**Convection** is the process by which heat travels through liquids and gases. Convection does not take place in solids.

## CONVECTION IN LIQUIDS

When a liquid is heated, the particles that it is made from gain heat energy, and move around more quickly. The liquid expands and its density decreases (see page 16). If the heat comes from one direction, the liquid nearest the heat becomes hot first. This rises through the denser, colder liquid around it, and takes the heat energy with it. The denser, colder liquid moves in to take its place. This in turn becomes warmer and less dense, and it rises. When the warm liquid reaches the top, it is pushed aside by more warm liquid rising. It cools and slowly falls, only to be heated and rise again.

This continuous process is called convection. The cyclical movement of the liquid creates a current called a **convection current**. Slowly, the temperature of all of the liquid will increase.

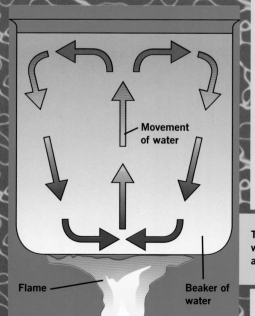

Movement of water

Flame

Beaker of water

This diagram shows how convection works. The cyclical movement is called a convection current.

# CONVECTION IN GASES

Convection works in the same way in gases as it does in liquids. As the gas is heated, it expands, becomes less dense, and rises. Colder, denser gas moves in to take its place, is heated, and rises. This explains why you can have cold feet in a hot room. A fire or heater warms the air, the hot air rises, and cold air is drawn in below it, which creates a cold draught around your feet. If you hold a spiral of paper above a warm radiator, it will turn as the warm air around it rises.

The burner in a hot-air balloon heats the air at the bottom of the balloon. The hot air expands and rises, and lifts the balloon.

# COOLING AND CONVECTION

Convection can also happen when an object is colder than the air around it. Heat energy moves from the air into the object. The loss of heat energy means that the air closest to the object is cooler and more dense than the surrounding air, and so it falls. Warm air moves in to take its place and a convection current begins.

## Did you know...?

The word "convection" comes from the Latin word *convehere*. This is made up from two Latin words, *con*, which means "together" and *vehere*, which means "to carry". It can help to make sense of what is going on in convection if you think about the liquid as a vehicle carrying the heat energy around.

# USING CONVECTION

Convection can be very useful both for heating and cooling our buildings. It can also cool engines and machines, as well as people.

# NATURAL CONVECTION

Heat from a fire or radiator will warm the air around it. The air becomes less dense and rises, and cooler, denser air takes its place. This in turn warms and rises, and a convection current begins, eventually warming the whole room. When the air currents arise naturally, without anything pushing the air to make it move, it is called natural convection.

# CONVECTION AND CHIMNEYS

An open fire in a house relies on convection. The air above the fire is heated. As it rises, carrying smoke up the chimney with it, cold air is drawn in at the base of the fire. A convection current begins as this in turn is heated by the fire, and rises, drawing in yet more cold air below.

# FORCED CONVECTION

It is possible to speed up convection by using a fan or pump to make the liquid or gas move more quickly than it would naturally. This is called **forced convection**, and it can be very useful. For example, a fan heater uses forced convection. A motor blows hot air towards you more quickly than a natural convection current would. In hot weather, we use forced convection when a fan blows cold air towards us, again more quickly than a natural convection current would.

**As cool air is blown by the fan, the strips of paper attached to the fan flutter in the convection current.**

# CONVECTION AND REFRIGERATION

Simple **refrigeration** systems use forced convection to cool the inside of the fridge. A system of pipes contains a fluid called a **refrigerant**. The refrigerant is pumped through the pipes, passing through a network called an **evaporator**. Here, it **absorbs** heat from the air in the fridge and carries it away, leaving the air cooler. The pressure of the refrigerant drops to keep the volume the same, so the refrigerant is pumped through a compressor, to restore its pressure. Next, it travels through a condenser where it loses its extra heat outside the fridge. After cooling, it is then ready to pass back to the evaporator to absorb more heat from the air in the fridge, and continue the cooling process.

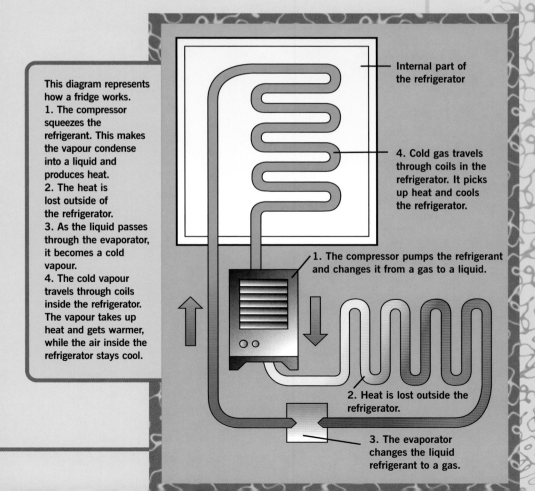

This diagram represents how a fridge works.
1. The compressor squeezes the refrigerant. This makes the vapour condense into a liquid and produces heat.
2. The heat is lost outside of the refrigerator.
3. As the liquid passes through the evaporator, it becomes a cold vapour.
4. The cold vapour travels through coils inside the refrigerator. The vapour takes up heat and gets warmer, while the air inside the refrigerator stays cool.

Internal part of the refrigerator

4. Cold gas travels through coils in the refrigerator. It picks up heat and cools the refrigerator.

1. The compressor pumps the refrigerant and changes it from a gas to a liquid.

2. Heat is lost outside the refrigerator.

3. The evaporator changes the liquid refrigerant to a gas.

# CONVECTION AND WIND

Heat from the Sun reaches all parts of Earth, but the temperature is higher at the equator than at the North and South Poles. This is because the equator is hit more directly by the Sun's rays.

Around the equator, the hot air expands and rises. The atmospheric pressure decreases because each gas particle takes up more space than it did when it was cold – the air becomes less dense.

Cold air from the Poles is more dense because the air particles are closer together. Dense, high-pressure air moves from the Poles towards the equator. It in turn is warmed and rises.

The warmed air slowly cools and becomes more dense. It falls away from the low pressure area around the equator and moves back towards the high pressure areas at the Poles. These air movements are winds. The movement of Earth spinning on its axis swings the winds sideways.

There are three main patterns of wind in each of Earth's hemispheres. The trade winds are around the equatorial regions, the polar winds are around the Poles, and the westerly winds are between them. These winds create the weather patterns around the globe.

Polar winds

Westerly winds

Equator

Trade winds

Polar winds

This map shows Earth's wind patterns. The pink arrows are the polar winds, the blue arrows are the westerly winds, and the orange arrows are the trade winds.

# THERMALS

Rising columns of warm air are called **thermals**. After many hours of sunshine, especially over rocky surfaces, these can reach more than 1 kilometre (0.6 miles) high. Birds can glide in these, using the rising air to lift them without having to expend their own energy. Humans can make use of thermals, too. Gliders are aeroplanes without engines. They are usually launched either by **winching**, or by being towed by another aircraft, and then released. Once in the air, the pilot glides slowly downwards without power, but can use thermals to regain lost height and stay airborne for longer.

# CONVECTION IN THE OCEANS

The Sun heats the water in areas of ocean around the equator. As winds blow across the surface of the oceans, they create ocean currents that push the warm water towards the Poles. As the warm water moves towards the Poles, it cools and sinks. Cold water from the Poles drifts in deeper ocean currents back towards the equator, where it in turn is heated, rises, and moves back towards the Poles again. These convection currents carry heat energy around the oceans and seas of Earth.

This map shows the main surface ocean currents on Earth. The red arrows indicate warm water, and the blue arrows indicate cold water.

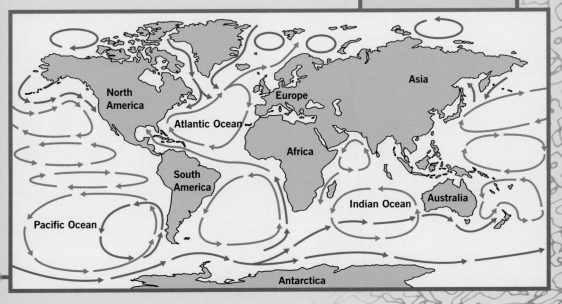

# Heat radiation

Radiation is the process by which heat energy travels as waves, similar to the way that light travels. **Heat radiation**, which is usually harmless, is not the same as nuclear radiation, which can be extremely dangerous.

The scientific name for heat radiation is **infrared** radiation. This is a type of electromagnetic wave that, together with other electromagnetic waves, such as visible light rays, **microwaves**, **x-rays**, and **radio waves**, makes up the **electromagnetic spectrum**. Infrared waves have longer **wavelengths** than visible light, but shorter wavelengths than microwaves. Infrared radiation is given off by anything that is hot. The hotter the object, the more infrared radiation it will give off.

The electromagnetic spectrum represents all the forms of electromagnetic radiation. Different forms of radiation are used in different ways.

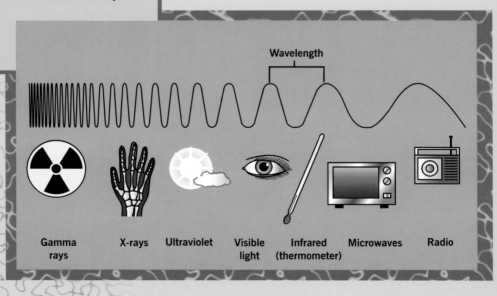

Wavelength

| Gamma rays | X-rays | Ultraviolet | Visible light | Infrared (thermometer) | Microwaves | Radio |

# TRAVELLING BY RADIATION

Unlike conduction and convection, radiation does not depend on the movement of particles. Like all electromagnetic waves, infrared waves are simply a movement of energy and nothing else. Infrared waves travel away from a hot object in straight lines in every direction. The speed of travel is the same as that of all electromagnetic waves – an amazing 300 kilometres (186 miles) per second! Because it is only energy that is moving, infrared radiation can travel through a **vacuum**. It can also travel through transparent materials such as glass.

# FEELING INFRARED RADIATION

When you stand in front of a hot object and feel the heat it gives off, you are feeling infrared radiation. Although convection currents carry heat energy around a room, the heat energy itself is infrared radiation. The heat energy travels from the object, through the space between it and you, and into your body. The nearer to the object you are, the greater the amount of infrared radiation that will reach you, and the hotter it will feel. For example, if you stand right in front of a fire, it feels hotter than if you stand at a distance from it.

## CASE STUDY  Infrared radiation in space

You might expect that the nearer a planet is to the Sun, the hotter it would be, but this is not always the case. Mercury, the planet nearest to the Sun, has an average daytime temperature of 420°C (788°F). Venus (see right), the next nearest planet to the Sun, has an average temperature of 464°C (867°F). Venus is actually hotter than Mercury. This is because Mercury has no atmosphere. There is nothing to block the infrared radiation from the Sun, but there is also nothing to prevent it escaping again either. Venus has a very dense, carbon-dioxide-rich atmosphere that behaves like the glass in a greenhouse. It allows most of the infrared radiation from the Sun in, but then prevents it escaping. Venus just gets hotter and hotter!

# INFRARED RADIATION AND MATERIALS

The surface of an object can affect the amount of infrared radiation the object **emits**. The emitted radiation then travels through the air until it hits another object. What happens next depends on the colour and texture of the object it hits:

• Emission – Identical objects with different surfaces will emit different amounts of infrared radiation. Dull, dark surfaces emit more infrared radiation than shiny, light surfaces.

• Absorption – Identical objects with different surfaces will absorb different amounts of infrared radiation. Dull, dark surfaces absorb more infrared radiation than shiny, light surfaces.

• Reflection – Identical objects with different surfaces will reflect different amounts of infrared radiation. Dull, dark surfaces reflect less infrared radiation than shiny, light surfaces.

# USING EMISSION, ABSORPTION, AND REFLECTION

The ways in which different surfaces affect the amount of infrared radiation emitted, absorbed, and reflected can be useful. For example, in hot countries, light-coloured clothing will keep a person cooler than dark clothing. This is because light colours reflect more, and absorb less, infrared radiation than dark colours. Painting buildings in hot countries white maximises the amount of heat they reflect, keeping the inside of the buildings as cool as possible.

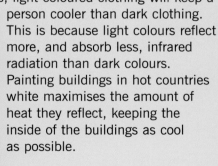

The majority of the houses in this village in Greece are painted white to reflect infrared radiation.

# KEY EXPERIMENT  Leslie's cube

The effect of colour and texture on the amount of infrared radiation emitted and absorbed can be seen from this experiment.

A Leslie's cube is a metal box with four sides painted differently: (a) dull black, (b) shiny black, (c) dull silver, and (d) shiny silver. Four thermometers, each attached to a stand, are placed at equal distances from the cube, one on each side, and the metal box is filled with hot water. The temperature shown by each thermometer is then read at regular intervals. Any change in temperature will be due to infrared radiation emitted from the surface that the thermometer faces.

The temperature will increase least rapidly in front of the shiny, silver surface, and most rapidly in front of the dull, black surface. This shows that shiny, light surfaces emit less infrared radiation than dull, dark surfaces.

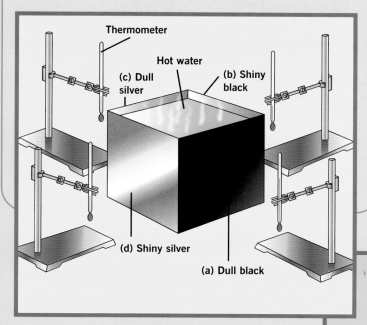

Thermometer

Hot water

(c) Dull silver

(b) Shiny black

(d) Shiny silver

(a) Dull black

This diagram shows the set up for the Leslie's cube experiment.

# COOKING WITH INFRARED RADIATION

If food is put under a grill, it cooks. This cannot happen by conduction because the grill does not touch the food, and the air between them is an insulator. It cannot happen by convection because hot air rises, and the food is beneath the grill. Therefore, the food must cook by the infrared radiation emitted from the hot grill.

## CASE STUDY  Microwave ovens

Microwave ovens cook food using microwaves. These waves are shorter than radio waves but longer than infrared waves. A tube called a **magnetron** generates microwaves, which are spread around the inside of the oven by a fan. In a normal oven, heat energy travels from the outside of the food to the centre by conduction. In a microwave, the microwaves cook food by making all the particles in the food vibrate at the same time. This means that food can be heated more quickly in a microwave oven than in a normal oven.

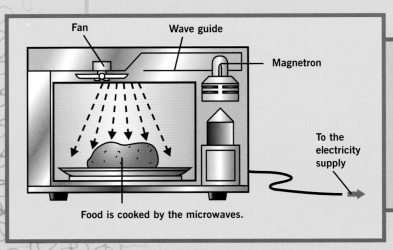

Fan

Wave guide

Magnetron

To the electricity supply

Food is cooked by the microwaves.

The magnetron produces the microwaves, which are guided into the main body of the oven by the wave guide. Once in the oven they bounce around off the surfaces and into the food.

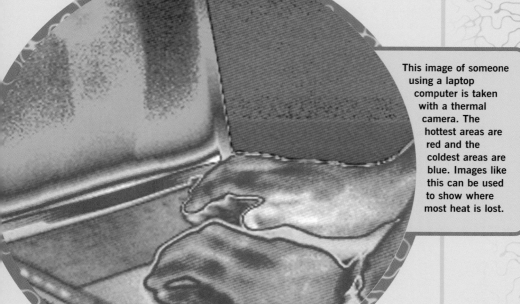

This image of someone using a laptop computer is taken with a thermal camera. The hottest areas are red and the coldest areas are blue. Images like this can be used to show where most heat is lost.

# THERMAL IMAGING

Anything that is warmer than its surroundings emits infrared radiation. A living body will emit infrared radiation because it is warmer than the air around it. Rescuers can use equipment with thermal sensors to locate survivors in disasters such as earthquakes.

Thermal imaging can also be used to provide "night vision". Thermal sensors do not need light to work. They can detect patterns of heat at night and give people, such as police and soldiers, the ability to "see" in the dark. Cameras that detect infrared radiation rather than light can be used to take images that show hot, warm, and cool areas. These cameras are called **thermographs**. They can be used in hospitals, and to detect where heat is being lost from buildings. Thermal images of Earth taken from satellites can be useful in weather forecasting.

# HEAT RADIATION AND ANIMALS

Warm-blooded animals, such as mammals and birds, are able to regulate their body temperature and keep it at a constant level. Cold-blooded animals, such as reptiles, are unable to do this. Instead, they rely on external factors for maintaining their body temperature. For example, lizards bask in sunshine to allow their bodies to absorb the infrared radiation from the Sun's rays. To maximise this, they align themselves so that they are facing in the direction of the Sun. They also expand their ribcage to increase their body surface area. Because dark colours absorb more infrared radiation than light colours, some lizards even change their skin colour from light to dark when basking.

# DESERT FOXES

Overheating can be a problem for animals that live in very hot climates. Some animals, such as desert foxes, lose heat through their ears! The fox's especially long ears provide a large surface area from which heat can travel into the air by conduction and radiation. Once in the air, the heat is carried away by convection.

The desert fox (below) is not the only animal whose large ears function as a cooling mechanism. Other animals, such as elephants and jack rabbits, also have large ears that help them keep cool in hot climates.

## CASE STUDY  The pit viper

Pit vipers, like most snakes, have poor eyesight and poor hearing. They are **carnivores**, and most of their hunting is done at night when vision is limited anyway. You might think it is difficult for them to find their prey, but they do this by detecting heat.

They have a pair of pits on each side of their head. These pits are covered with a temperature-sensitive **membrane**. The membranes can detect the infrared radiation given off by a warm-blooded animal.

Using this sense, pit vipers can detect their prey from a distance of up to half a metre (1.6 feet). Their heat-detecting sense even helps pit vipers to keep cool. They can locate cool areas in which to rest when they begin to get too hot.

This Sumatran pit viper senses heat from its prey.

# EARTH AND RADIATION

The Sun constantly emits vast amounts of infrared radiation. About 40 per cent of the infrared radiation that travels towards Earth is reflected straight back into space by the atmosphere and the land surfaces. About 15 per cent is absorbed by the atmosphere. Only about 45 per cent actually warms the planet.

In the Arctic and Antarctic, snow and ice reflect more than 90 per cent of the infrared radiation that reaches them. In these regions, the air is extremely cold because very little of the infrared radiation from the Sun is retained.

# Storing and saving heat

Anything that gives out heat is called a heat source. The Sun is the major heat source for Earth. Without heat energy and light energy from the Sun, Earth would be a cold, dark place where no living thing could exist.

The Sun is a natural heat source – it is not man-made. Another natural heat source is Earth itself. Deep below the solid crust, the rocks of our planet are extremely hot. This heat energy contained below Earth's surface is called **geothermal energy**. It is this heat source that heats the water that bubbles out of hot springs in Iceland and New Zealand.

**The Sun is Earth's most important source of infrared radiation (heat).**

## SCIENCE PIONEERS Joule, Mayer, and Helmholtz: Energy transfer

In 1847, three scientists working independently each came up with the same idea. The scientists were James Joule, Julius Mayer (1814–78), and Hermann Ludwig Helmholtz (1821–94). Their idea became known as the Law of the Conservation of Energy. It states that "Energy cannot be created or destroyed". This means that the only way of getting heat energy is by changing one form of energy into another. Changing energy from one type to another is called an **energy transfer**.

# HEAT FROM ENERGY TRANSFERS

Other types of energy can be transferred into heat energy.
Some are shown in this table:

| Type of energy | Source | How it is transferred into heat energy |
|---|---|---|
| **Chemical energy** | **Fossil fuels** (oil, coal, and gas)<br><br>**Biofuels** (wood, **biomass**, and biogas) | Some fuels are burned in power stations to make electricity. The electricity is used to power appliances, such as electric fires and cookers. Some fuels are burned directly, such as in gas cookers, gas fires, and oil-fired boilers. |
| Kinetic (movement) energy | Wind (moving air)<br><br>Water (waves, rivers) | The kinetic energy in moving air or water is used to drive machinery that makes electricity, which is then used to power appliances such as electric fires and cookers. |
| Potential energy | High-level dams that hold water back | When the dam is opened, water rushes downwards, and potential energy is changed to kinetic energy that can be used in the ways described above. |
| **Nuclear energy** | Locked inside atoms | In nuclear power stations, nuclear reactions release the nuclear energy within atoms. This is used to produce electricity that can be used in the ways described above. |

# FOSSIL FUELS AND SAVING ENERGY

Many of our power stations use fossil fuels – coal, oil, and gas – to produce electricity. We use electricity to power heating systems, cookers, and other heat-giving appliances. Fossil fuels take millions of years to form. Modern, industrialized societies use them at an astonishing rate, and most scientists agree that these fuels will eventually be used up. By reducing the amount of energy we waste, we can make our fossil fuel resources last longer. This is one good reason for saving heat energy.

# ENVIRONMENTAL CONCERNS

Many different environmental concerns have been raised with regard to energy:

• **Pollution** – Using some forms of energy, particularly fossil fuels, creates pollution that causes environmental damage, such as air pollution caused by car exhausts. Burning fossil fuels can also contribute to health problems such as asthma and other respiratory conditions.

• Nuclear waste – Using nuclear energy to create electricity does not cause pollution in the same way that fossil fuels do, but it does produce nuclear waste. As yet, there are no satisfactory ways to store or dispose of nuclear waste. Many scientists feel that nuclear waste is a huge potential environmental hazard.

• Climate change – Global warming and the greenhouse effect are just two of the terms heard on news bulletins around the world. They describe the changes that many scientists predict will damage our world forever. These are in many ways caused by our excessive energy use.

# HOW IS HEAT ENERGY WASTED?

Heat energy can be wasted in several ways. Many machines and appliances are inefficient. This means that they use more energy to do a particular job than they need to. Lack of insulation can cause heat energy to be lost from buildings. For example, walls, windows, doors, and roofs all let heat escape by conduction. Heat energy can be wasted more generally by people simply using more heat energy than they need to.

# HOW CAN HEAT ENERGY BE SAVED?

Some problems can only be tackled by governments, large companies, and research establishments. However, each individual can reduce the amount of heat energy they waste.

• Inefficiency – New appliances, such as ovens and heaters, now show efficiency ratings. This makes it easy to choose the most efficient model when replacing old, worn-out appliances.

• Insulation – Ensuring a house is well-insulated reduces its heat loss. Loft insulation, cavity wall insulation, double glazing, and draught excluders can all help to save heat energy.

• Waste – Making daily choices, such as putting on a sweater instead of a thin T-shirt, means you can turn the central heating temperature down, and use less energy. Shutting doors and windows prevents heat escaping. Boiling just enough water for a mug of coffee instead of heating a whole kettle-full saves heat energy.

Saving heat energy is something we can all do, and there is a direct benefit for us too. As well as helping the environment, reducing the amount of heat energy we use reduces our fuel bills. Saving energy also means saving money.

Entire wall made from glass to let in sunlight for warmth.

This building is very energy-efficient. It has one wall made from glass, which lets in warmth from the Sun. This reduces the amount of central heating that is needed. Where possible, the building is made from recycled materials.

# STORING HEAT ENERGY

For hundreds of years, fossil fuels have been the traditional source of heat energy for our homes. Today, modern technology enables us to make more use of the natural heat energy from the Sun. Trapping and storing the Sun's energy can reduce the use of fossil fuels, which could make our resources last longer, and reduce pollution and environmental damage.

# TRAPPING ENERGY FROM THE SUN

Energy from the Sun is called solar energy. An enormous amount reaches the surface of Earth. In one day, every square metre (11 square feet) of Earth's surface receives the same amount of energy as would be contained in one barrel of oil. Until recently, virtually all of this energy was wasted. With modern technology, though, it can be trapped and used.

Solar panels fixed on the roofs of buildings can be used to heat water or to generate electricity. In simple panels designed to heat water, a pump circulates cold water through a network of pipes beneath the panels. When sunlight hits the panels, its heat energy warms the water in the pipes. The warmed water travels away from the panels and is stored in a tank for later use.

## RECENT DEVELOPMENTS  Into the future

An innovative project in the United States is developing ABE technology. This stands for Active Building Envelope, which is a system that uses solar energy to provide both heating and cooling. It consists of solar panels, thermostatic heat pumps, and a storage device. The system automatically controls the temperature in an enclosed space. It uses solar energy to heat it if it begins to get cold, and cool it if it begins to get hot. Scientists hope that the system could be incorporated into building surfaces, taking the place of traditional heating and air-conditioning systems. The technology may eventually be extended to other applications, such as self-cooling drinks bottles!

Alternatively, the warm water is passed through radiators to heat the inside of the building. More complex systems can concentrate the solar energy to produce temperatures as high as 3,000°C (5,430°F). This heat can be used in industry, or in the production of electricity.

Solar cells can also produce electricity directly. They have two layers of silicon crystals, each with another chemical added to increase electrical conductivity. When sunlight hits the cell, its energy makes electrons flow between the layers, creating an electric current.

## SO WHAT DOES IT ALL MEAN?

Most scientists agree that fossil fuels will not last forever, and so we should try to minimise energy waste. Some of the innovative, new, pollution-free approaches to energy generation will help. In the future, even more approaches will be developed, and every one of us can help by reducing our energy consumption and waste.

The solar panels on the roof of ths house use energy from the Sun to produce electricity.

# Further resources

## MORE BOOKS TO READ

*Everyday Science: Turning up the Heat: Energy*, Ann Fullick (Heinemann Library, 2004)

*Fascinating Science Projects: Energy and Heat*, Bobbi Searle (Franklin Watts, 2002)

*Science Files: Heat and Energy*, Steve Parker (Heinemann Library, 2005)

*Science World: Heat and Energy*, Kathryn Whyman (Franklin Watts, 2003)

## USING THE INTERNET

Explore the Internet to find out more about heat. You can use a search engine, such as www.yahooligans.com or www.google.com, and type in keywords such as heat energy, thermal, change of state, water cycle, fossil fuel, solar energy, or nuclear energy.

These search tips will help you find useful websites more quickly:

• Know exactly what you want to find out about first.

• Use only a few important keywords in a search, putting the most relevant words first.

• Be precise. Only use names of people, places, or things.

# Glossary

**absolute zero**   lowest possible temperature (0 degrees Kelvin, −273.15°C, −459.67°F)

**absorb**   soak up

**atmospheric pressure**   force with which air presses down

**atom**   smallest unit of matter

**bimetal strip**   strip made from pieces of two different metals

**biofuel**   fuel made from biological materials

**biomass**   living mass of plants

**boiling point**   temperature at which a liquid turns into a gas

**buckling**   bending out of shape

**carnivore**   animal that hunts and eats other animals

**chemical energy**   energy held inside a substance

**condensation**   change in state from a gas to a liquid

**condense**   change state from a gas or vapour to a liquid

**conduction**   mechanism by which heat energy travels through solids

**conductor**   material that allows heat or electricity to pass

**contract**   get smaller, take up less space

**convection**   transfer of heat by circulation through a gas or liquid

**convection current**   flow of air or water that transfers heat

**current**   flow of a substance or energy

**degree Celsius (°C)**   standard unit for measuring temperature

**density**   measure of the amount of a substance in a given space; how tightly packed the particles are

**deposition**   change directly from gas to solid

**distortion**   bending or twisting out of shape

**electromagnetic spectrum**   full range of waves of energy

**electron**   negatively charged particle in an atom

**emit**   give off

**energy**   ability to make something happen or change

**energy transfer**   change from one type of energy to another. The change from chemical energy to light energy when a battery torch is turned on is an energy transfer.

**ethanol**  liquid that can be used in thermometers

**evaporate**  change state from a liquid to a gas or vapour

**evaporation**  change in state from liquid to gas or vapour

**evaporator**  equipment that causes change from a liquid to a gas or vapour

**expand**  get bigger, take up more space

**forced convection**  circulation of gas or liquid that is started or speeded up by a fan or pump

**fossil fuel**  source of energy, such as oil, natural gas, and coal, formed millions of years ago from the remains of living things

**freeze**  change state from a liquid to a solid

**freezing point**  temperature at which a liquid changes to a solid

**furnace**  enclosed space in which heat is produced by burning fuel

**gas**  state in which particles are free to fill the space available

**geothermal energy**  energy from inside Earth itself

**heat**  form of energy

**heat radiation**  transfer of heat energy as waves

**heat sink**  device that conducts and disperses heat

**infrared**  type of electromagnetic energy; heat radiation

**insulator**  material that does not allow heat or electricity to pass

**joule**  unit of energy

**kinetic energy**  energy of moving things

**liquid**  substance that flows but keeps the same volume; state in which particles are not held in a regular shape, but are not completely free

**magnetron**  device that generates microwaves

**mass**  measure of the amount of matter in a substance

**melt**  change state from a solid to a liquid

**melting point**  temperature at which a substance changes from a solid to a liquid

**membrane**  thin, skin-like layer

**microprocessor**  control circuit inside a computer that processes information

**microwave**  type of electromagnetic energy

**molecule**  substance composed of two or more atoms joined together

**neutron**  neutral particle in an atom

**nuclear energy**  energy released when atoms are split or fused

**particle**  atom or molecule; one of the tiny parts from which everything is made

**pollution**　damage to the environment by the addition of something harmful or unpleasant

**potential energy**　energy stored in an object that can change to kinetic (movement) energy

**precipitation**　water falling from clouds as rain, snow, or hail

**pressure**　force with which one thing presses on another

**proton**　positively charged particle in an atom

**radio wave**　type of radiation that can be used for communication

**reflect**　bounce off

**refrigerant**　substance used to provide cooling

**refrigeration**　keeping something colder than its surroundings

**solid**　substance that has a definite size and shape; state in which particles are held together in a fixed arrangement

**sublimation**　change directly from a solid to a gas

**temperature**　measure of how hot or cold something is

**thermal**　relating to heat

**thermal conductor**　substance that allows heat energy to travel through it easily

**thermal insulator**　substance that does not allow heat energy to travel through it easily

**thermals**　large columns of hot or warm air rising from the ground

**thermograph**　camera showing patterns of heat

**thermometer**　instrument used to measure temperature

**thermostat**　device that controls an appliance by responding to its temperature

**transpiration**　process by which plants lose water from their leaves into the atmosphere

**vacuum**　completely empty space

**variable**　something that can be changed

**vent**　window-like device that opens and closes

**vibrate**　shake; move very quickly to and fro

**volume**　amount of space occupied by a substance

**wavelength**　length of a wave from one peak to the next

**winch**　haul or lift using a powerful machine

**x-ray**　type of radiation that can go through some substances, allowing objects, such as bones and organs in the body, to be photographed

# Index